# SCARY SCENES
## FOR

# Scary Scenes
# for
# Halloween

## JiLL WILLIAMS GROVER

Sterling Publishing Co., Inc.  New York
A Sterling/Chapelle Book

Chapelle, Ltd.:
- Owner: Jo Packham
- Editor: Laura Best
- Illustrator: Pauline Locke
- Photo Stylist: Jill Grover
- Staff: Marie Barber, Ann Bear, Areta Bingham, Kass Burchett, Rebecca Christensen, Dana Durney, Holly Fuller, Marilyn Goff, Holly Hollingsworth, Sherry Hoppe, Shawn Hsu, Susan Jorgensen, Barbara Milburn, Linda Orton, Karmen Quinney, Leslie Ridenour, Cindy Stoeckl

If you have any questions or comments, please contact:
Chapelle, Ltd., Inc., P.O. Box 9252, Ogden, UT 84409
(801) 621-2777 • (801) 621-2788 Fax • chapelle1@aol.com

Library of Congress Cataloging-in-Publication Data

Grover, Jill Williams
    Scary Scenes for Halloween / Jill Williams Grover.
        p.    cm.
    "A Sterling/Chapelle book."
    ISBN 0-8069-4842-6
    1.  Halloween decorations.   2.  Handicraft.   3.  Halloween cookery.
I. Title.
TT900.H32G78    1999
    745.594' I--dc21                                                99-18590
                                                                         CIP

10 9 8 7 6 5 4 3 2 1

Published by Sterling Publishing Company, Inc.
387 Park Avenue South, New York, NY 10016
©1999 by Chapelle Ltd.
Distributed in Canada by Sterling Publishing
c/o Canadian Manda Group, One Atlantic Avenue, Suite 105
Toronto, Ontario, Canada M6K 3E7
Distributed in Great Britain and Europe by Cassell PLC
Wellington House, 125 Strand, London WCR2 0BB, England
Distributed in Australia by Capricorn Link (Australia) Pty Ltd.
P.O. Box 6651, Baulkham Hills, Business Centre, NSW 2153, Australia
Printed in Hong Kong
All Rights Reserved

Sterling ISBN 0-8069-4842-6

This book is dedicated to my children Laci, Levi, and River, who fill my Halloween and my life with rewarding tricks and beautiful treats.

Special thanks to
John and Shirley Valcarce
of Perry, Utah,
for supplying pumpkins and gourds to enhance our scary halloween ideas.

# About the Author

I have loved Halloween over the years for many different reasons. Fall is when life seems to slow down a bit—I like when family seems to snuggle in for the winter.

When I was little, I remember carefully planning the homes that I would visit. This decision was not based on the candy they would give but the feeling or memory of the year before.

The front porch decorations had a lot to do with it. I was always curious about a quick peek inside the home. I'll never forget this scary old witch sitting in an old rocking chair on her porch scaring at least half of the trick or treaters away. Her house was always my favorite because if you made it past her she would invite you into her home which was filled with the true spirit of Halloween; hot cider, a warm glowing fire, and a real scary witch with a big heart and smile. This is when I learned a lot about life. "Things aren't usually what they seem." Happy Halloween!

Jill and her husband Richard live in Brigham City, Utah, with their three children—Laci, Levi, and River. Jill works as an interior designer decorating all over the world.

# Halloween Origins

### Colors
In ancient time, black stood for death and night. Orange stood for the harvest, and was also the color of the fire used to keep demons away.

### Jack-o-Lanterns
The Irish tell a story about a man named Jack. He was so bad, he could not go to heaven. In hell, he played too many tricks and the devil sent Jack away. Jack had nowhere to go. All he owned was a little lantern. The Irish called him "Jack of the Lantern."

### Costumes
The Celts believed the god Samhain came to earth on October 31, which was their New Year's Eve. He let the dead come back with him. Out of fear, the Celts made big fires and burned animals as gifts. Some Celts wore costumes made from animals' heads and furs.

### Trick-or-Treating
In past Ireland, people believed in ghosts. Irish farmers went to rich homes and asked for food. If rich people gave no food, the farmers played tricks on them, like stealing a gate or moving a wagon far away. Rich people thought ghosts had played the tricks and began giving food to the farmers.

# TABLE OF

## SCARY NIBBLES

## ENTER AT YOUR OWN RISK

# CONTENTS

## FRIGHTFUL FEAST

## GOBLIN GATHERING

SCARY NIBBLES

# Ghost Lamp

*Pictured on page 8*

## Materials:

Black acrylic paint
Clear packing tape
Light bulb, 25 watt
Old lamp with harp, min. 30" H
White plastic ball, 10"-dia.
White spray paint
White twin sheet

## Tools:

Paintbrush

## Instructions:

1. Paint lamp with white spray paint. Let dry.

2. Refer to Ghost Lamp Diagram 1. Attach white plastic ball to top of lamp harp with packing tape.

3. Place light bulb in lamp.

4. Refer to Ghost Lamp Diagram 2. Center and drape white twin sheet over top of ball.

5. Paint eyes on front of sheet with black acrylic paint, using paintbrush.

**Ghost Lamp Diagram 1**

**Ghost Lamp Diagram 2**

# Bugs & Hisses

## Pictured on page 12

## Materials:

Aluminum screen, 6" square
Black acrylic paint
Canning jar with ring
Chocolate candy kisses
Paper tag with black string
Plastic bugs, snake, spiders

## Tools:

Black felt-tip marker
Foam brush
Matches

## Instructions:

1. Paint canning ring with black acrylic paint, using foam brush. Brush sides of jar with black acrylic paint.

2. Fill jar with chocolate kisses, and plastic bugs and spiders.

3. Write on paper tag: "Hugs and Kisses—Bugs and Hisses", using black felt-tip marker.

4. Burn edges of tag, using matches. Do not let burn more than 2–3 seconds. Tie tag around jar with black string.

5. Place screen square on top of jar and secure with black canning ring. Wrap plastic snake around jar.

A plastic mummy case can be used in place of canning jar. After candy is gone, the Bugs & Hisses jar makes a "nice" bug collector.

# Scary Treat Bucket

## Pictured on page 12

## Materials:

Black spray paint
Brown acrylic paint
Candy
Red nail polish
Small galvanized
  bucket

## Tools:

Latex gloves

## Instructions:

**1.** Spray bucket with black spray paint, letting some silver show through. Let dry.

**2.** Apply brown acrylic paint on one palm of latex-gloved hands. Rub hands together and gently pat bucket.

**3.** Drizzle red nail polish down sides.

**4.** Fill bucket with candy.

*To use the Scary Treat Bucket as a Halloween centerpiece, fill bucket with tomato soup and plastic bones. Add dry ice for added effect.*

# Hand Full of Candy

*Pictured on page 14*

## Materials:

Black acrylic paint
Black sheer nylon ribbon,
  1½"-wide (36")
Black toile ribbon (36")
Jaw breakers
Latex glove
Plastic fingertips
Red squeeze paint
Spider ring

## Tools:

Small paintbrush
Transfer tool

## Instructions:

1. Fill latex glove with jaw breakers. Tie closed with black ribbons and tie in a bow.

2. Transfer Hand Full of Candy Stitches Pattern onto glove, using transfer tool.

3. Paint stitches on glove with red paint, using paintbrush. Let dry.

4. Paint nails of plastic fingertips with black acrylic paint.

5. Place plastic fingertips on glove. Place spider ring on one finger.

**Hand Full of Candy Stitches Pattern**

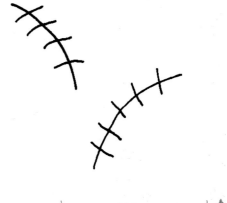

# Candy Candle

*Pictured on page 16*

## Materials:

Candle
Candy pumpkins
Ceramic pot

## Instructions:

1. Place candle inside ceramic pot.

2. Surround candle with candy pumpkins.

*Tip: Spiders crawling around the candle will add a scarier effect.*

# Candy Wrapper Bucket

## Pictured on page 18

## Materials:

Black acrylic paint
Candy
Candy wrappers
Découpage medium
Small galvanized bucket

## Tools:

Foam brush
Latex gloves

## Instructions:

1. Apply enough découpage medium on bucket, using foam brush, to cover size of a candy wrapper. Place wrapper on découpage medium surface and smooth with fingers to remove bubbles.

2. Continue to adhere candy wrappers until bucket is covered. Apply a final coat of découpage medium over entire bucket. Let dry.

3. Apply black acrylic paint on one palm of latex-gloved hands. Rub hands together and gently pat bucket. Let dry.

4. Fill bucket with candy.

*Do not limit surprises to candy; Candy Wrapper Buckets can be filled with a variety of holiday favors.*

Reese's
2 PEANUT BUTTER CUPS
Reese's
2 PEANUT BUTTER CUPS
Reese's
2 PEANUT BUTTER CUPS
PEANUT BUTTER CUPS

# Yummy Mummies

*Pictured on page 18*

## Materials:

Cereal Mixture
Gauze, 1½"-wide (36")
Plastic wrap
Round suckers
White curling ribbon

## Tools:

Black felt-tip marker
Cooking spray
Scissors

---

### Cereal Mixture

*Pictured on page 18*

½ cup butter or margarine
4 cups miniature marshmallows
3 cups crispy rice cereal
3 cups frosted oat cereal
1 cup white chocolate baking chips

1. In a large saucepan, melt butter over low heat. Add marshmallows. Using a wooden spoon, stir until melted. Remove from heat.

2. Stir in crispy rice and frosted oat cereals. Let sit for 10 minutes. Add white chocolate baking chips.

---

## Instructions:

1. Apply cooking spray to hands. Gather a handful of cereal mixture.

2. Refer to Yummy Mummies Diagram 1. Push sucker into center of cereal mixture and form a round ball.

3. Wrap cereal ball with plastic wrap. Twist and wrap down around sucker stick.

4. Refer to Yummy Mummies Diagram 2. Wrap sucker with strip of gauze.

5. Draw two dots for eyes, using black felt-tip marker.

6. Tie white ribbon around plastic wrap and sucker stick and curl, using scissors.

**Yummy Mummies Diagram 1**

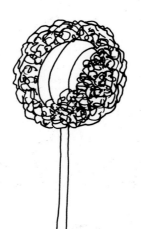

**Yummy Mummies Diagram 2**

# Skeleton Jug

*Pictured on page 20*

## Materials:

Adhesive remover
Black acrylic paint
Candy
Dish soap
Small plastic jug

## Tools:

Butter knife
Latex gloves
Paintbrushes: craft, liner
Transfer tool

*Skeleton Jugs placed around an old tree give a spooky illumination.*

## Skeleton Jug Pattern

## Instructions:

1. Wash empty jug with soapy water. Remove stickers with adhesive remover.

2. Transfer Skeleton Jug Pattern onto jug, using transfer tool.

3. Paint skeleton eyes and nose with black acrylic paint, using craft paintbrush.

4. Paint lid black if it is a color other than orange. Paint mouth, using liner paintbrush. Let dry.

5. Scrape some paint off, using butter knife, giving a worn effect.

6. Apply black acrylic paint on palm of latex-gloved hands. Rub hands together and gently pat jug.

7. Fill jug with candy.

# Ghost Sticks

*Pictured on page 22*

## Materials:

Almond bark candy
Candy corn
Candy eyes
Chocolate candy kisses
Large pretzel sticks
Orange sprinkles

## Tools:

Microwave
Microwave-safe bowl
Waxed paper

## Instructions:

1. Melt almond bark candy, following package directions, using microwave and microwave-safe bowl.

2. Roll pretzels in melted almond bark to coat. Place on waxed paper. Place two candy eyes on each pretzel and let set.

3. For variety, add orange sprinkles and top with a chocolate candy kiss.

4. For jagged effect, roll pretzel in almond bark, let set for 2 minutes then roll again.

# Fence for Ghost Sticks

*Pictured on page 22*

## Materials:

Black jelly beans
Dry ice
Picket fence pot
Scary rubber hands (2)
Water

## Tools:

Bread tin
Small pan

## Instructions:

1. Fill bread tin with black jelly beans. Set bread tin inside picket fence pot.

2. Place scary rubber hands on either side of bread tin.

3. Fill small pan with dry ice and water; place under bread tin.

4. Add Ghost Sticks to bread tin.

# Masked Pumpkin

*Pictured on page 24*

## Materials:

Black acrylic paint
Black mask
Medium fresh pumpkin
Votive candle

## Tools:

Craft knife
Felt-tip marker
Matches
Spoon

## Instructions:

1. Cut off top of pumpkin, using craft knife. Save top for lid.

2. Scoop out seeds and fiber from pumpkin, using spoon, and discard.

3. Refer to Masked Pumpkin Diagram 1. Place black mask around pumpkin. Mark eye holes, using felt-tip marker.

4. Remove mask. Cut out eye holes, using craft knife. Replace lid.

5. Refer to Masked Pumpkin Diagram 2. Drizzle black acrylic paint down pumpkin.

6. Place mask back on pumpkin, lining up mask and pumpkin eye holes.

7. Place candle inside pumpkin and light, using matches.

**Masked Pumpkin
Diagram 1**

**Masked Pumpkin
Diagram 2**

# Toile Jewel Pumpkin

## Pictured on page 26

## Materials:

Large fresh pumpkin
Plastic spiders
Ribbon
Small craft jewels
Toile fabric

## Tools:

Hot-glue gun & glue sticks
Scissors

## Instructions:

1. Wrap fresh pumpkin with piece of toile fabric. Tie top with ribbon or excess toile.

2. Adhere jewels on toile and ribbon, using hot-glue gun.

3. Adhere plastic spiders randomly around pumpkin.

*To welcome Halloween friends, an invisible man can be "enhanced" with a Toile Jewel Pumpkin and a steaming cup of spiced apple cider.*

# Witch Hat

*Pictured on page 29*

## Materials:

Black toile ribbon
Bubble wrap
Chicken wire ribbon
Raw sienna acrylic paint
Witch hat

## Tools:

Craft scissors
Hot-glue gun & glue sticks
Matches
Paintbrush

## Instructions:

1. Stuff hat with bubble wrap.

2. Refer to Witch Hat Diagram 1. Cut chicken wire ribbon to fit around base of hat, using craft scissors.

3. Burn holes in black ribbon, using matches.

4. Weave black toile ribbon in and out of chicken wire ribbon. Leave ends long enough to tie around hat.

5. Refer to Witch Hat Diagram 2. Adhere woven ribbons to hat, using hot-glue gun.

6. Brush patches randomly around hat with raw sienna acrylic paint, using paintbrush.

**Witch Hat Diagram 1**

**Witch Hat Diagram 2**

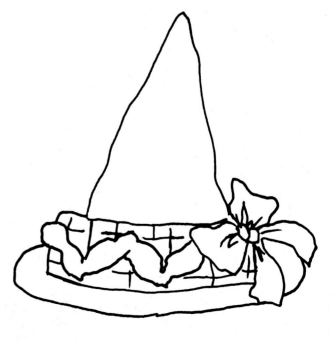

# Broomstick

*Pictured on page 29*

## Materials:

Acrylic paints: black, orange
Black plastic spider
Black sheer nylon ribbon (36")
Black spray paint
Black toile ribbon (36")
Broom

## Tools:

Foam brush
Hot-glue gun & glue sticks
Latex gloves
Masking tape, 2"-wide
Matches

## Instructions:

1. Paint entire broom with black spray paint. Let dry.

2. Refer to Broomstick Diagram. Wrap strips of masking tape around broom handle every 2".

3. Paint open sections on handle with orange acrylic paint, using foam brush. Let dry; remove tape.

4. Apply black acrylic paint on one palm of latex-gloved hands. Rub hands together and gently pat broom handle.

5. Tie black ribbons to lower handle end of broom.

6. Burn holes in ribbon, using matches. Refer to photo on page 29 for placement.

7. Adhere plastic spider to ribbon, using hot-glue gun.

*A spiderweb draped over the Broomstick can add a scary Halloween effect.*

# Witch Shoes

*Pictured on page 29*

## Materials:

Black rust preventive spray paint
Black toile ribbon
Modeling clay
Old shoes
Paper cups, 8 oz. (2)

## Tools:

Craft scissors
Hot-glue gun & glue sticks

## Instructions:

1. Cut off rim of paper cups, using craft scissors.

2. Refer to Witch Shoes Diagram 1. Adhere paper cup to toe of each shoe, using hot-glue gun.

3. Form modeling clay around cup until smooth to make long pointed toes. Let dry for three days.

4. Refer to Witch Shoes Diagram 2. Remove shoelaces from shoes. Create squiggles randomly around outside of shoes to add texture, using hot-glue gun.

5. Spray shoes with black spray paint.

6. Lace shoes with black toile ribbon.

**Witch Shoes Diagram 1**

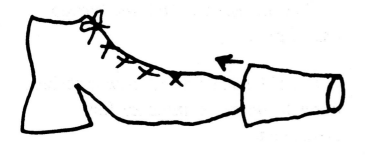

**Witch Shoes Diagram 2**

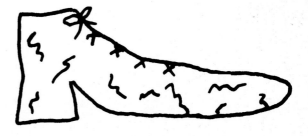

*"Designer" witches know shoes can be a Halloween color other than black.*

# Photo Wreath

Pictured on page 32

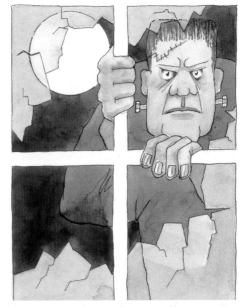

When decorating doors, do not forget adding to windows.

## Materials:

Black acrylic paint
Black sheer nylon ribbon
Black spray paint
Color copies of Halloween photographs
  of family and friends
Laminate sheets
Grapevine wreath
Spiders
Spiderweb
White burlap ribbon
White toile ribbon

## Tools:

Hot-glue gun & glue sticks
Latex gloves
Matches
Paper hole punch

## Instructions:

1. Spray wreath with black spray paint.

2. Cover color copies of photographs with laminate sheets. Make a small hole at the top of each photo, using paper hole punch.

3. Burn around edges of each photograph copy, using matches. Burn holes in black nylon ribbon and white toile ribbon.

4. String black ribbon through paper-punched holes and attach photographs to wreath.

5. Make large bows with white toile and white burlap ribbons.

6. Adhere bows, spiders, and spiderweb to wreath, using hot-glue gun.

7. Apply black acrylic paint on one palm of latex-gloved hands. Rub hands together and gently pat white ribbons.

Tip: The photo wreath can go on the front door—so all of last year's trick or treaters can see themselves in costume from the previous year. You may choose to take the photo of a child off the wreath and give it to him or her when coming to visit you.

33

# Poppin' Walkway

### *Pictured on page 35*

## Materials:

Acrylic paints: black, blood red
Big shoes with
   aggressive tread
Bright red nail polish
Bubble wrap, 6' long
Carpet runner, 6' x 27"

## Tools:

Craft scissors
Foam brush
Latex gloves

## Instructions:

**1.** Apply black acrylic paint on one palm of latex-gloved hands. Rub hands together and gently pat carpet.

**2.** Paint soles of shoes with blood red acrylic paint, using foam brush. Place shoes on runner and press firmly. Alternate shoes along runner to suggest walking.

**3.** Drip blood red acrylic paint along runner. Let dry. Apply bright red nail polish over red paint to add texture.

**4.** Cut bubble wrap to same size as runner, using craft scissors. Place bubble wrap underneath runner. Place runner on walkway and porch leading to front door.

*The Poppin' Walkway is a good way to announce spooky Halloween guests.*

# Dead Tree

## Pictured on page 35

## Materials:

Black latex spray paint (aluminum paint is not safe with lights)
Black plastic flower pot, 12"-dia.
Concrete mix
Dead branches
Floral wire
White Christmas lights, 35–light strand

## Tools:

Latex gloves

## Instructions:

1. Spray paint dead branches with black spray paint. Let dry.

2. Mix concrete in flower pot, following manufacturer's instructions.

3. Place dead branches upright in concrete and support until set.

4. Beginning with light closest to pronged plug, wrap strand of lights around branches. Secure strand to branches with floral wire.

5. Wearing latex gloves, cover light bulbs while spraying branches and light cord with black latex spray paint.

*Dead branches can be substituted for bones of a spooky scarecrow.*

# Trick or Treat Pillowcase

## Pictured on page 35

## Materials:

Fabric paints: black, red
Halloween photo
Heat transfer
Newspaper
Paper plate
White pillowcase

## Instructions:

1. Take Halloween photo to professional copy store and have a heat transfer created.

2. Take photo heat transfer to a T-shirt printing store and have transfer ironed onto pillowcase.

3. Line inside of pillowcase with newspaper to prevent paint from bleeding inside. Have child smear palm of hand with black fabric paint then stamp on pillowcase. Let dry.

4. Drizzle red fabric paint to look like blood.

For the month of October, the Trick or Treat Pillowcase can be used on "child's bed." On Halloween night, it can be used for trick-or-treating.

# Witch Hat Luminary

*Pictured on page 39*

## Materials:

Black spray paint
Incense cones (3)
Incense holder
PVC traffic cone, 28", available at
  industrial supply stores

## Tools:

Compact floodlight

**Witch Hat Luminary
Diagram**

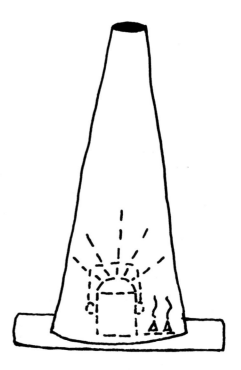

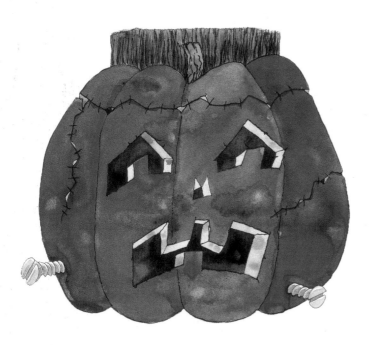

*Incense cones can also be placed inside
lit Jack o' Lanterns.*

## Instructions:

1. Spray traffic cone with 2–3 coats of black spray paint. Let dry.

2. Refer to Witch Hat Luminary Diagram. Place incense cones on holder and place underneath traffic cone. Place floodlight under traffic cone.

3. Use luminaries to light walkway to front door.

# Holy Pumpkin

Pictured on page 39

**Materials:**

Black spray paint
Compact floodlight
Large fresh pumpkin

**Tools:**

Craft knife
Electric drill & ¾" drill bit
Spoon

**Instructions:**

1. Cut opening in bottom of pumpkin, using craft knife.

2. Scoop out seeds and fiber from pumpkin, using spoon, and discard.

3. Refer to Holy Pumpkin Diagram. Randomly drill holes all over pumpkin, using drill & ¾" drill bit.

4. Place compact floodlight inside pumpkin.

# Black Pumpkin

Pictured on page 39

**Materials:**

Black spray paint
Compact floodlight
Large fresh pumpkin

**Tools:**

Craft knife
Electric drill & ¾" drill bit
Spoon

**Instructions:**

1. Cut opening in bottom of pumpkin, using craft knife. Spray pumpkin with black spray paint. Let dry.

2. Refer to Holy Pumpkin Diagram. Randomly drill holes all over pumpkin, using drill & ¾" drill bit.

3. Place compact floodlight inside pumpkin.

**Holy Pumpkin Diagram**

# Skeleton Topiary

*Pictured on page 39*

## Materials:

1-gal. plastic jug
Black acrylic paint
Black latex spray paint (aluminum
   paint is not safe with lights)
Black sheer nylon ribbon (36")
Black spray paint
Black toile ribbon
Black tricot fabric, 20" x 36"
Dowel, 1" x 36"
Floral wire
Florist foam blocks (2)
Galvanized bucket, 9" tall
White Christmas lights, 35-light
   strand

## Tools:

Butter knife
Foam brush
Hot-glue gun & glue sticks
Latex gloves
Matches

## Instructions:

1. Lightly spray bucket with black spray paint to give a smoky effect.

2. Paint face on jug with black acrylic paint, using foam brush. After face is dry, scrape some paint off, using butter knife, giving a worn effect.

3. Apply black acrylic paint on one palm of latex-gloved hands. Rub hands together and gently pat jug.

4. Adhere two foam blocks together, using hot-glue gun. Adhere blocks to inside of bucket. Push dowel into foam.

5. Refer to Skeleton Topiary Diagram 1 on page 42. Beginning with light closest to pronged plug, wrap strand of lights around dowel from bottom to top, pushing remaining lights into jug.

6. Secure strand to dowel with floral wire.

7. Spray dowel and light cord with black latex paint.

8. Adhere jug to dowel, using hot-glue gun.

9. Burn holes in black toile and nylon ribbon, using matches.

10. Wrap black ribbons around neck of jug and tie in bows.

11. Refer to Skeleton Topiary Diagram 2. Drape and adhere black tricot onto jug head, using hot-glue gun.

12. Adhere black excelsior inside bucket.

**Skeleton Topiary Diagram 1**

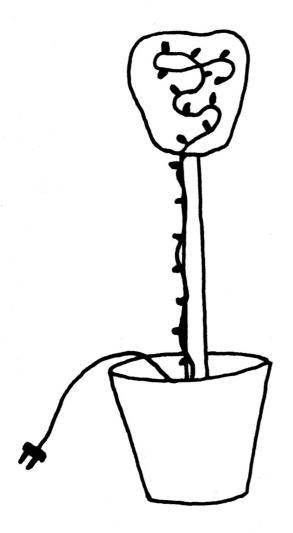

**Skeleton Topiary Diagram 2**

# Flying Bats

*Pictured on page 43*

## Materials:

Black acrylic paint
Black spray paint
Black toile ribbon, 5½" x 19"
Foam sheet
Hair & body glitter spray
Wire, 26-gauge
Wire clothes hanger

## Tools:

Craft scissors
Hot-glue gun & glue sticks
Matches
Paintbrush
Stapler & staples

## Instructions:

**1.** Refer to Flying Bat Diagram 1. Straighten hook of hanger. Squeeze top and bottom wire of hanger together on each side and secure with 26-gauge wire.

**Flying Bat
Diagram 1**

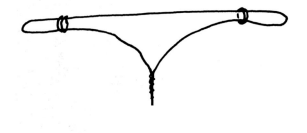

**Flying Bat
Diagram 2**

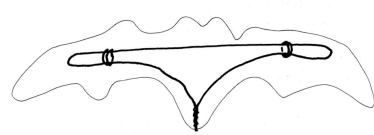

**Flying Bat
Pattern**

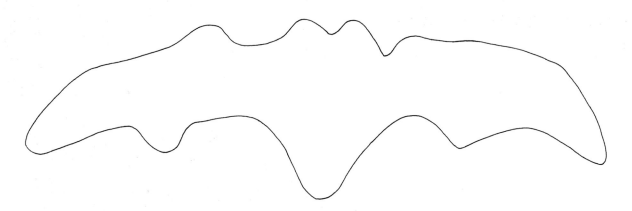

2. Spray hanger with black spray paint. Let dry.

3. Lay Flying Bat Pattern onto foam sheet and cut around it, using craft scissors.

4. Refer to Flying Bat Diagram 2. Adhere foam to hanger, using hot-glue gun. Bend hanger as necessary so no wire is seen from the front.

5. Burn holes in ribbon, using matches. Refer to photo on page 43 for placement.

6. Lay ribbon on top of bat. Make two tucks in ribbon by bat ears and staple 1" from top. Staple rest of bat to foam.

7. Cover staples with black acrylic paint, using paintbrush.

8. Spray bat with hair and body glitter to give sparkle and extra dimension.

*Bats on a rickety old fence can add a haunted feel to any Halloween house.*

# Black Moss Chair

*Pictured on page 46*

## Materials:

Black spray paint
Old chair
Spanish moss

## Tools:

Hot-glue gun & glue sticks
Leather gloves

## Instructions:

1. Adhere Spanish moss sporadically over chair, especially in spots that have been worn, wearing leather gloves and using hot-glue gun.

2. Spray chair with 3–4 coats of black spray paint, covering moss and chair.

3. Place Invisible Man in chair or fill chair with pumpkins, a black cat, or trick or treat buckets filled with candy.

# Invisible Man

*Pictured on page 46*

## Materials:

Chair
Chrome-colored enamel spray paint
Fish line or heavy-gauge wire
Glasses
Hat

## Tools:

Hot-glue gun & glue sticks

## Instructions:

1. Spray hat and glasses with 2–3 coats of chrome-colored spray paint. Let dry.

2. Refer to Invisible Man Diagram. Adhere glasses to hat at an angle, using hot-glue gun, to suggest someone is wearing them. Spray paint over glued area.

3. Using heavy-gauge wire, secure invisible man to a chair; OR, using fishing line, suspend invisible man from ceiling.

**Invisible Man Diagram**

Hat brim

# Spiderweb Invitations

*Pictured on page 50*

## Materials:

Black construction paper, 8½" x 11"
Black jewelry thread
Black rust preventive spray paint
Halloween printed clear cellophane
Spider confetti
Spiderweb
Spray adhesive
White copy paper, 8½" x 11"
White high quality paper
White mailing tube
White marbled translucent paper,
   8½" x 11"

## Tools:

Black felt-tip marker
Clipboard
Matches
Needle

## Instructions:

1. Find an actual incredible spiderweb outdoors without the spider. Spray web with black spray paint.

2. Place quality paper on clipboard. Spray paper with adhesive spray. Place paper behind web and gently scoop web forward to attach to paper.

3. Size web to fit 8½" x 11" paper. Copy web onto translucent paper.

4. Write party invitation on white 8½" x 11" copy paper, using black felt-tip marker.

5. Burn around edges of translucent paper with copy of web, copy paper with invitation, and black construction paper, using matches.

6. Layer translucent, white, and black papers. Refer to photo on page 50 for placement. Secure layers in top left-hand corner with 4—5 spaced stitches, using needle and thread.

7. Scorch around mailing tube, using matches. Place invitation in mailing tube along with some spider confetti.

8. Spray tube with adhesive. Cut printed cellophane to fit. Pull cellophane tightly around tube to seal. Mail invitation.

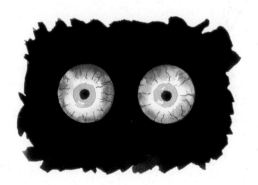

*A spooky face could be substituted for the spiderweb.*

# Spider Tablecloth

## Pictured on page 52

### Materials:

Netting or toile, size of table
  with 12" overhang
Plastic spiders, 2"

### Tools:

Fabric scissors
Needle & thread
Table

### Instructions:

1. Hem netting, using needle and thread.

2. Place netting on table, then place settings on table.

3. Insert each spider's legs into holes of netting until table is overrun with spiders.

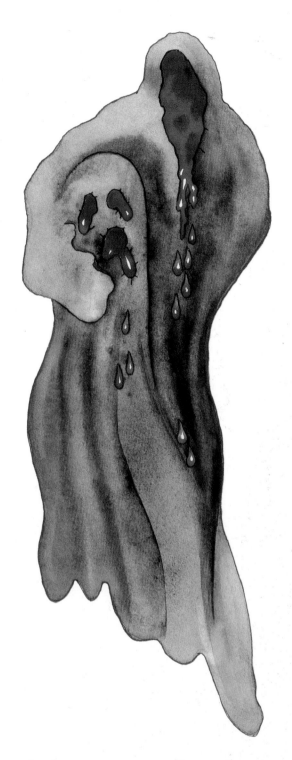

*Leftover netting can be made into ghosts and hung in corners.*

# Black Mask Candle

*Pictured on page 54*

## Materials:

Black mask
Black, oil-based spray paint
Candleholder
Water
White candle

## Tools:

Bucket
Hot-glue gun & glue sticks
Latex gloves

*Use a bat mask as an alternative cover.*

## Instructions:

1. Fill bucket with water, enough to submerge entire candle. Spray top of water with three or four squirts of black spray paint.

2. Refer to Black Mask Candle Diagram. Completely immerse white candle upside down in water and paint mixture, using latex gloved hands.

3. Pull candle out and let dry upright.

4. Paint candleholder with black spray paint. Let dry.

5. Adhere candle into candleholder, using hot-glue gun. Be careful not to melt candle.

6. Place black mask around candle. Pull string tight and tie to secure.

**Black Mask Candle Diagram**

# Dripping Candles

*Pictured on page 56*

## Materials:

Candleholder
Household wax, 16 oz.
Spanish moss
White spray paint
White taper candles (5)

## Tools:

Latex gloves
Matches
Measuring cup
Newspaper
Old crockpot

## Instructions:

1. Melt household wax in crockpot. Let cool about 20 minutes after melting.

2. Place Spanish moss on newspaper and spray with white spray paint.

3. Place candles in candleholder. Place candleholder on newspaper. Light candle, using matches, and let burn for 5 minutes.

4. Drape Spanish moss around candleholder.

5. Measure out ½ cup of melted wax, wearing latex gloves. Slowly drip wax at top of candle (do not cover wick) and over Spanish moss. Repeat until desired effect is achieved. Be certain to pour wax slowly. The drips collect better when you pour slowly.

*Coffins make a great centerpiece along with Dripping Candles.*

# Spiderweb Art

*Pictured on page 59*

## Materials:

Adhesive spray
Black mat for framing
Black rust preventive spray paint
Frame
High quality paper
Spiderweb
Spray adhesive

## Tools:

Clipboard

## Instructions:

1. Find an actual incredible spiderweb without the spider.

2. Spray spiderweb with black spray paint.

3. Place high quality paper on clipboard. Spray paper with spray adhesive.

4. Go behind spiderweb with paper and gently scoop spiderweb forward to attach to paper.

5. Mat and frame spiderweb.

*A broken window could be used as the frame for Spiderweb Art.*

# spiderweb Glass

*Pictured on page 60*

## Materials:

Glass

## Tools:

Masking tape
White accent pen

## Instructions:

**1.** Tape copy of Spiderweb Pattern to inside of glass.

**2.** Trace over pattern on outside of glass with white accent pen.

**3.** Remove pattern.

**Spiderweb Pattern**

# Spider Ice Cubes

*Pictured on page 60*

## Materials:

Dish soap
Rubber spiders (16)
Water

## Tools:

Freezer
Ice cube tray

## Instructions:

**1.** Clean rubber spiders with dish soap in warm water; rinse well. Place spider in each section of ice cube tray.

**2.** Cover each spider with water. Make certain a spider remains in each tray section. Place ice cube tray in freezer and allow cubes to freeze solid.

*Tip: If using ice cubes in drinks, please remind childhood guests that spiders should not be swallowed!*

# Black Charger

*Pictured on page 62*

## Materials:

Black chalkboard spray paint
White chalk
Wooden chargers (one for
  each guest)

## Instructions:

**1.** Spray chargers with
3–4 coats black spray
paint. Let dry.

**2.** Write a Halloween
message on each charger
with white chalk.

*Scary pictures can be drawn on Black
Charger, rather than a written message.*

## Clear Drink

*Pictured on page 62*

Lemon lime soda
White grape juice

1. Mix equal parts lemon lime soda and white grape juice.

## Dracula's Bow Tie Pasta

*Pictured on page 62*

12 oz. bow tie pasta
1 Tbl. olive oil
2 cloves garlic, thinly sliced
4 roma tomatoes, peeled and diced
Leaves of 1 bunch fresh basil, thinly sliced
⅓ cup chicken broth
Salt and pepper to taste
¾ cup freshly grated parmesan cheese

1. Cook bow tie pasta in a large pot of boiling salted water for about 13 minutes.

2. Heat olive oil in medium skillet over medium heat. Saute garlic until lightly brown.

3. Add tomatoes, basil, and chicken broth. Cook 3 minutes. Sprinkle with salt and pepper.

4. Place pasta in serving bowl and toss with sauce and parmesan cheese.

* low fat dish

# Flower Pot Place Card

## Pictured on page 65

## Materials:

Black, oil-based spray paint
Dowel, ⅛"-dia. (8")
Name tag
Spanish moss
Styrofoam, 2½"-dia.
Terra cotta pot, 2½"-dia.
White flower pick

## Tools:

Black felt-tip
  marker
Craft glue
Hot-glue gun &
  glue sticks
Matches

## Instructions:

1. Adhere styrofoam inside pot, using craft glue.

2. Adhere small amount of Spanish moss to styrofoam.

3. Insert dowel and stem of pick into styrofoam. Spray dowel, pick, and pot with black spray paint.

4. Write name on tag, using black felt-tip marker. Burn edges of tag, using matches.

5. Adhere name tag to dowel, using hot-glue gun.

Another interesting place card is made to represent a tombstone with the guest's name incorporated in the epitaph.

# Bat Napkin

*Pictured on page 65*

## Materials:

Black square cloth napkin
Pipe cleaners (3)

## Instructions:

1. Fold dinner napkin into quarters.

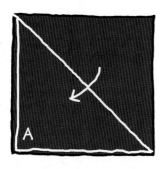

2. Fold back first flap (A).

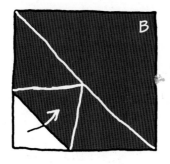

3. Fold point A back to center.

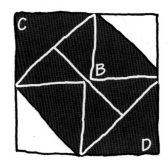

4. Fold second flap (B) to center.

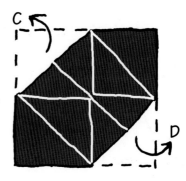

5. Fold C & D toward back and meet in center back.

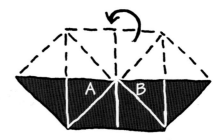

6. Fold napkin in half with A & B on top.

7. Place edges on bottom. Squeeze and wrap center with pipe cleaner. Twist to secure.

8. Fold pipe cleaner in center, then in quarters to create bat ears. Repeat with another pipe cleaner.

9. Twist both pipe cleaners together.

10. Repeat Steps 8 and 9 to other side of bat ear.

# Miniature Gourds

*Pictured on page 68*

## Materials:

Découpage medium
Gourds

## Tools:

Foam brush

## Instructions:

1. Apply one coat découpage medium to each gourd, using foam brush, leaving shiny finished look.

*Miniature Gourds can accent "empty" places in the home--from the stairway, to table, to porch.*

# Scary Gift Wrap

## Pictured on page 70

**Materials:**

Black toile ribbon
Color copy of photograph to fit
  top of box
Découpage medium
Halloween wrapping paper
Sturdy box

**Tools:**

Cellophane tape
Foam brush

**Instructions:**

1. Wrap box and lid separately, using Halloween wrapping paper and cellophane tape.

2. Apply découpage medium on top of box, using foam brush.

3. Place color copy of photograph on découpage medium and smooth with hand to remove air bubbles. Refer to photo for placement.

4. Apply découpage medium on top of photograph, using foam brush. Let dry.

5. Tie black ribbon around box and tie in a bow.

Tip: After using as a gift box, this makes a great storage box for special treasures. Children love getting a gift with their photo on it.

# Chalkboard Frame

## Pictured on page 70

**Materials:**

Black chalkboard spray paint
Halloween photograph, size of frame
Picture frame with 1"-wide edge
White chalk

**Instructions:**

1. Remove backing and glass from frame.

2. Spray frame with at least 3–4 coats of black spray paint. Let dry between coats.

3. Reassemble frame with glass, photograph, and backing.

4. Write a Halloween greeting on edge of frame with white chalk.

GOBLIN
GATHERING

# Witch Hat Place Card

*Pictured on page 74*

## Materials:

Black, oil-based spray paint
Black pipe cleaner
Black raffia
Black ribbon (6")
Decorative cupcake liner
Green pepper
Green plastic eyes, 18 mm, (1 pair)
Heavyweight place card
Paper cup, 8 oz.
Small rubber spider
Small witch hat
White toile, 6" square

## Tools:

Black felt-tip marker
Craft scissors
Hot-glue gun & glue sticks
Nail
Ruler

## Instructions:

1. Make hole in tip of witch hat, using nail.

2. Refer to Witch Hat Place Card Diagram 1. Tie a knot in one end of pipe cleaner and push untied end up through hole from inside hat.

3. Apply hot glue to knot, using hot-glue gun, and pull pipe cleaner up and tight, adhering knotted pipe cleaner to inside of hat.

4. Cut toile into a circle. Cut ¼"-dia. hole in center of toile.

5. Refer to Witch Hat Place Card Diagram 2 on page 75. Place toile over hat, stringing pipe cleaner through hole. Refer to photo on page 74 for placement. Tie black ribbon around base of hat, securing toile. Trim toile edges around hat, using craft scissors.

## Witch Hat Place Card
### Diagram 2

## Witch Hat Place Card
### Diagram 3

**6.** Cut black raffia into 12" strands, using craft scissors. Bundle strands together. Tie bundle into knot close to one end, leaving enough length to create short bangs for witch's hair. Trim front raffia to create bangs.

**7.** Adhere knotted raffia around inside rim of hat, using hot-glue gun.

**8.** Adhere hat with hair to green pepper. Sometimes a green pepper will stand up better when turned upside down.

**9.** Carefully push green plastic cat eyes through front of green pepper.

**10.** Fill paper cup with water. Spray one or two squirts of black spray paint in cup of water.

**11.** Dip entire place card into cup of water, pull out, and let dry.

**12.** Handwrite guest's name on place card in a squiggle print (for a scary effect), using black felt-tip marker.

**13.** Refer to Witch Hat Place Card Diagram 3. Adhere printed place card to back of spider, using hot-glue gun. Adhere spider and card to end of pipe cleaner.

**14.** Place witch's head on a flattened decorative cupcake liner.

# Pot of Frankenstein

## Pictured on page 77

## Materials:

Conduit screw connectors (2)
Green plant pot, 9"-dia.
Potting soil
Rye grass

## Tools:

Hot-glue gun & glue sticks
Silver fine-tip felt marker

## Instructions:

1. Refer to Pot of Frankenstein Diagram and Optional Eye Diagram. Draw face and stitches on front of pot, using silver fine-tip felt marker.

*Grass will take 7-10 days to grow. After that, Frank will need a haircut now and then.*

2. Adhere conduit screw connectors onto sides on pot, using hot-glue gun.

3. Plant rye grass in pot with potting soil.

**Pot of Frankenstein
Diagram**

**Optional Eye
Diagram**

# Pot Dracula

*Pictured on page 77*

## Materials:

Black pot
Black plastic eyes (2)
Elijah blue festuca
Potting soil
Royal metallic brilliant silver paint

## Tools:

Accent liner pens: black, white
Hot-glue gun & glue sticks
Paintbrush
Transfer tool

## Instructions:

1. Transfer Pot Dracula Pattern onto pot, using transfer tool.

2. Paint face with royal metallic brilliant silver, using paintbrush. Let dry.

3. Adhere black plastic eyes, using hot-glue gun.

4. Paint mouth with black and teeth with white accent pens. Let dry.

5. Plant festuca in pot with potting soil.

**Pot Dracula Pattern**

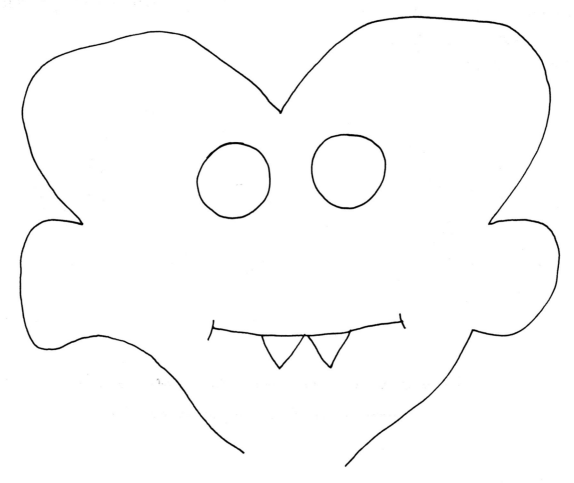

# Witch Pot

*Pictured on page 77*

## Materials:

Green plant pot, 9"-dia.
Potting soil
Sprenger's asparagus fern
Witch nose

## Tools:

Black fine-tip felt marker
Hot-glue gun & glue sticks
Transfer tool

## Instructions:

1. Transfer Witch Pot Pattern to front of plant pot, using transfer tool. Trace over transferred pattern, using black felt-tip marker.

2. Adhere witch nose to face on pot, using hot-glue gun.

3. Plant asparagus fern in pot with potting soil.

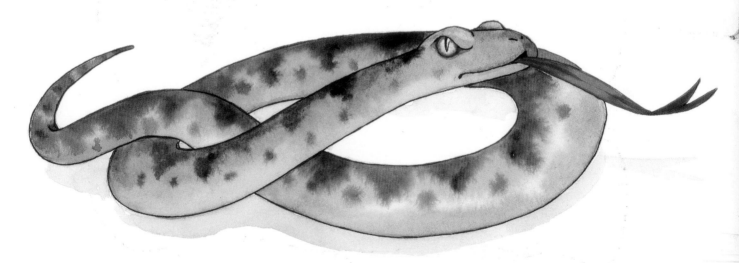

*Surround the pot with a scary plastic spider, or have one coming out of the pot for an added effect.*

# Candy Corn Candle Pot

*Pictured on page 80*

## Materials:

Acrylic paints: orange, white, yellow
Candy corn
Styrofoam circle, 6"-dia.
Terra cotta pot, 7"-dia.
Yellow candle, 4"-dia. (8")

## Tools:

Foam brush
Hot-glue gun & glue sticks
Masking tape
Ruler

## Instructions:

**1.** Refer to Candy Corn Candle Pot Diagram 1. Wrap masking tape around pot, 2½" up from bottom.

**2.** Paint bottom of pot with yellow, using foam brush. Paint rim of pot with white. Let dry.

**3.** Wrap masking tape around top edge of yellow bottom.

**4.** Paint middle of pot with orange. Let dry.

**5.** Apply hot glue around rim of styrofoam circle, using hot-glue gun. Place styrofoam circle inside pot.

**6.** Refer to Candy Corn Candle Pot Diagram 2. Center and adhere bottom of candle to top of styrofoam circle.

**7.** Fill pot with candy corn.

**Candy Corn Candle Pot
Diagram 2**

# Cyclopes Mug

## Cyclopes Mug Diagram

*Pictured on page 82*

## Materials:

Black decorating frosting
Fruit-chew candies
Mug
Roll candies
White frosting

## Tools:

Butter knife

## Instructions:

1. Dab white frosting on roll candies, using butter knife. Then attach to mug. Dab frosting on fruit-chew candy and attach to roll candies. Refer to Cyclopes Mug Diagram. Dot eye with black decorating frosting.

2. Repeat this process until mug is randomly covered.

---

### Mandarin Cream Soda

*Pictured on page 82*

1 liter cream soda
2 cans mandarin orange slices
1 gallon orange juice

1. Place 3 orange slices in each section of ice cube tray. Cover oranges with orange juice. Freeze until solid.

2. Place 3 orange juice cubes in each glass, then fill with cream soda.

---

### Candy Corn Chowder

*Pictured on page 82*

5 slices bacon
1 med. onion, thinly sliced
3 med. potatoes, pared and diced
Water
1 box frozen honey-glazed carrots
1 pkg. white sauce mix
1 (17 oz.) can cream-style corn
1 tsp. salt
Dash pepper

1. In a large frying pan, cook bacon until crisp. Crumble and set aside. Reserve 3 Tbl. bacon drippings in pan.

2. Add onion and cook until light brown. Add potatoes and carrots. Add enough water to cover.

3. Cook over medium heat 10–15 minutes, until potatoes and carrots are cooked.

4. Cook white sauce, following package instructions. Stir in cream-style corn, salt, and pepper. Add to potato and carrot mixture and heat through about 10 minutes.

5. Top each serving with crumbled bacon.

Makes 6 servings

# Frankenstein Cake Cone

*Pictured on page 84*

## Materials:

Black decorating frosting in tube
Candy eyes
Chocolate cake mix
Chocolate frosting
Green ice cream cone, flat-bottomed
Licorice roll candy: black with orange
Peanut butter cup
Small green candies

### Frankenstein Cake Cone Diagram 1

### Frankenstein Cake Cone Diagram 2

## Tools:

Butter knife
Mixing bowl
Mixing spoon
Oven

## Instructions:

1. Prepare chocolate cake mix, following package instructions.

2. Fill ice cream cone ½ full of cake batter and bake, following cupcake instructions on package. Let cool.

3. Apply chocolate frosting on top of baked cones, using butter knife.

4. Remove paper from one peanut butter cup and place on top of frosting. Let set.

5. Refer to Frankenstein Cake Cone Diagram 1. Make stitches from top of cone down the "head" at an angle with black frosting.

6. Attach candy eyes and make mouth with black frosting.

7. Attach one small green candy to each side of cone with black frosting. Let set.

8. Refer to Frankenstein Cake Cone Diagram 2. Attach small slice of licorice roll to green candy with black frosting.

# Napkin Candles

## Pictured on page 86

## Materials:

Black acrylic paint
Découpage medium
Glass jar
Halloween napkin or tissue paper
Orange glitter nail polish
Votive candle

## Tools:

Foam brush, 1½"
Latex gloves
Matches

## Instructions:

**1.** Cover outside of jar with découpage medium, using foam brush.

**2.** If napkin is 2-ply, tear outside layer off for a sheer effect.

**3.** Place napkin or tissue paper around jar; pat down softly. Let dry.

**4.** Apply découpage medium over outside of jar. Let dry.

**5.** Apply black acrylic paint on one palm of latex-gloved hands. Rub hands together and gently pat jar.

**6.** Drizzle black acrylic paint and orange glitter nail polish down sides of jar.

**7.** Place votive inside jar and light, using matches.

*Drawing a scary picture on the side of the votive sends an eerie look into the room when candle is lit.*

# Olive Fingers

## Pictured on page 88

## Materials:

Bowl
Jumbo black olives (2 cans)
Small latex gloves (2)
Water

## Tools:

Freezer

## Instructions:

1. Fill latex gloves with water. Tie knot in end of each glove. Freeze until solid.

**Olive Fingers Diagram**

2. Remove gloves from freezer. Add an olive to tip of each finger.

3. Refer to Olive Fingers Diagram. Place gloves in bowl, fingers up.

4. Pour remaining olives in bowl surrounding gloves.

*Even unexpected Halloween guests will love this treat.*

# Candy Garland

*Pictured on page 90*

## Materials:

Black-wrapped candy
Ribbon, length of table perimeter plus
    enough to tie on candies

## Tools:

Stapler

## Instructions:

1. Refer to Candy Garland Diagram 1. Attach each piece of candy to ribbon with one knot.

2. Refer to Candy Garland Diagram 2. Staple garland outside of Kids' Paper Tablecloth.

**Candy Garland Diagram 1**

**Candy Garland Diagram 2**

# Kids' Paper Tablecloth

*Pictured on page 90*

## Materials:

Black toile, twice the distance from
    table to floor
Butcher paper, to table dimensions
    plus 3" overhang
Crayons
Pipe cleaners

## Tools:

Stapler

## Instructions:

1. Lay butcher paper evenly over tabletop.

2. Fold toile in half lengthwise. Staple toile around inside bottom edge of butcher paper. Tucks can be made giving the appearance of gathers.

3. Secure Candy Garland to butcher paper around table sides, using stapler.

4. Wrap crayons with pipe cleaners. Set crayons randomly around table for children to color scary pictures.

# Fast Photo Place Mat

*Pictured on page 90*

### Materials:

Black heavy cardstock, 12" x 19"
Laminate sheets
Photo booth photo strip of each child
   in costume

### Tools:

All-purpose glue
Craft scissors

### Instructions:

1. Refer to Fast Photo Place Mat Diagram. Adhere photo strip along 12" side of black cardstock with all-purpose glue.

2. Laminate cardstock. Trim excess from edges, using craft scissors.

**Fast Photo Place Mat Diagram**

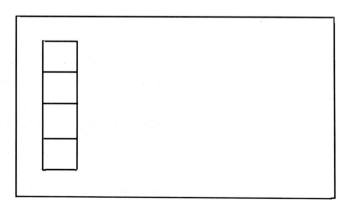

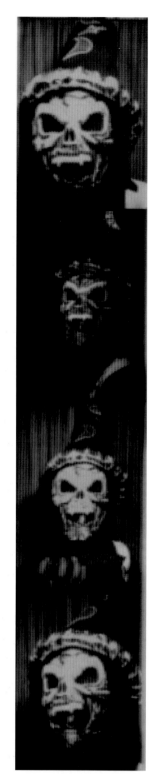

# Halloween Party Recipes

## Creamy Chicken Baked in a Pumpkin

1 small pumpkin
2 lbs. boneless chicken breast, cut into strips
1 can cream of celery soup
1 can cream of chicken soup
½ cup sour cream
Salt and pepper to taste
2 Tbl. sesame seeds
1 Tbl. butter
1 bundle green onions, sliced

1. Slice off ¼ top of pumpkin. Clean out seeds. Save top to use as lid.

2. Brown chicken in pan. Set aside.

3. Saute sesame seeds and green onion in butter. Take off heat. Add soups, sour cream, and salt and pepper.

4. Pour mixture into cleaned pumpkin. Replace lid and place on baking sheet. Bake at 350° for 1½ hours. Serve warm. Do not forget to scoop some pumpkin inside with each serving.

* Can be served over bed of pasta.

## Mom's Pumpkin Pie

4 eggs, slightly beaten
1 can pumpkin pie filling
1½ cup sugar
1 tsp. salt
1 tsp. cinnamon
½ tsp. ginger
¼ tsp. cloves
2 cups milk

1. Mix ingredients in order given and pour mixture in unbaked pie crust.

2. Bake at 425° for 15 minutes. Reduce oven to 350°; continue baking for 45 minutes or until knife comes out clean.

Makes two 9" pies

## Pie Crust

4 cups sifted all-purpose flour
1 tsp. salt
2 tsp. baking powder
½ cup shortening
¼ cup hot water
½ cup butter
1 tsp. lemon juice
1 egg yolk, beaten

1. Sift flour, salt, and baking powder together. Cut in shortening. Combine hot water with butter and lemon juice, then beat in egg yolk. Mix into dry ingredients. Chill. Use as required.

Makes two 9" pies

## Pumpkin Bars

2 cups pumpkin
4 eggs, beaten
1 cup oil
2 cups sifted all-purpose flour
1 cup brown sugar
1 cup sugar
¼ tsp. salt
1 tsp. baking powder
1 tsp. baking soda
1½ tsp. cinnamon
½ tsp. cloves
½ tsp. nutmeg

1. Blend pumpkin, eggs, and oil in a mixing bowl. Blend all the dry ingredients together, then fold into pumpkin mixture.

2. Pour onto a greased 9" square cake pan. Bake in a preheated 350° oven for 20–25 minutes.

3. Remove from the oven and cool to room temperature before frosting with Cream Cheese Frosting.

Makes 20 bars

## Cream Cheese Frosting

3 oz. cream cheese, softened
½ cup butter
½ cup powdered sugar
½ tsp. vanilla
1½ tsp. light cream

1. Mix cream cheese with butter. Whip in sugar, vanilla, and light cream. Spread over Pumpkin Bars.

## Pumpkin Muffins

¾ cup packed brown sugar
¼ cup molasses
½ cup soft unsalted butter
1 egg, beaten
1 cup canned pumpkin
1¾ cups flour
1 tsp. baking soda
¼ tsp. salt
¼ cup chopped pecans

1. In a medium bowl, cream sugar, molasses, and butter. Add eggs and pumpkin and blend well.

2. In another bowl, mix flour with baking soda and salt; then beat into pumpkin mixture. Fold in pecans.

3. Fill well-greased muffin pans half full with batter. Bake at 375° for 20 minutes.

Makes 16 muffins

## Herbed Pumpkin Bowl

1 small fresh pumpkin
¼ cup melted butter
Salt, pepper, and thyme to taste

1. Preheat oven to 400°. Cut pumpkin top off. Scrape seeds and pulp with spoon.

2. Lightly brush pumpkin with melted butter. Sprinkle with salt, pepper, and thyme to taste. Bake for 30–40 minutes until tender.

3. Fill pumpkin with whipped potatoes or favorite soup and serve warm.

Makes 1 serving

# Conversion Charts

## Inches to Millimetres and Centimetres

| Inches | MM | CM | Inches | CM | Inches | CM |
|---|---|---|---|---|---|---|
| ⅛ | 3 | 0.9 | 9 | 22.9 | 30 | 76.2 |
| ¼ | 6 | 0.6 | 10 | 25.4 | 31 | 78.7 |
| ⅜ | 10 | 1.0 | 11 | 27.9 | 32 | 81.3 |
| ½ | 13 | 1.3 | 12 | 30.5 | 33 | 83.8 |
| ⅝ | 16 | 1.6 | 13 | 33.0 | 34 | 86.4 |
| ¾ | 19 | 1.9 | 14 | 35.6 | 35 | 88.9 |
| ⅞ | 22 | 2.2 | 15 | 38.1 | 36 | 91.4 |
| 1 | 25 | 2.5 | 16 | 40.6 | 37 | 94.0 |
| 1¼ | 32 | 3.2 | 17 | 43.2 | 38 | 96.5 |
| 1½ | 38 | 3.8 | 18 | 45.7 | 39 | 99.1 |
| 1¾ | 44 | 4.4 | 19 | 48.3 | 40 | 101.6 |
| 2 | 51 | 5.1 | 20 | 50.8 | 41 | 104.1 |
| 2½ | 64 | 6.4 | 21 | 53.3 | 42 | 106.7 |
| 3 | 76 | 7.6 | 22 | 55.9 | 43 | 109.2 |
| 3½ | 89 | 8.9 | 23 | 58.4 | 44 | 111.8 |
| 4 | 102 | 10.2 | 24 | 61.0 | 45 | 114.3 |
| 4½ | 114 | 11.4 | 25 | 63.5 | 46 | 116.8 |
| 5 | 127 | 12.7 | 26 | 66.0 | 47 | 119.4 |
| 6 | 152 | 15.2 | 27 | 68.6 | 48 | 121.9 |
| 7 | 178 | 17.8 | 28 | 71.1 | 49 | 124.5 |
| 8 | 203 | 20.3 | 29 | 73.7 | 50 | 127.0 |

## Yards to Metres

| Yards | Metres | Yards | Metres | Yards | Metres | Yards | Metres | Yards | Metres |
|---|---|---|---|---|---|---|---|---|---|
| ⅛ | 0.11 | 2⅛ | 1.94 | 4⅛ | 3.77 | 6⅛ | 5.60 | 8⅛ | 7.43 |
| ¼ | 0.23 | 2¼ | 2.06 | 4¼ | 3.89 | 6¼ | 5.72 | 8¼ | 7.54 |
| ⅜ | 0.34 | 2⅜ | 2.17 | 4⅜ | 4.00 | 6⅜ | 5.83 | 8⅜ | 7.66 |
| ½ | 0.46 | 2½ | 2.29 | 4½ | 4.11 | 6½ | 5.94 | 8½ | 7.77 |
| ⅝ | 0.57 | 2⅝ | 2.40 | 4⅝ | 4.23 | 6⅝ | 6.06 | 8⅝ | 7.89 |
| ¾ | 0.69 | 2¾ | 2.51 | 4¾ | 4.34 | 6¾ | 6.17 | 8¾ | 8.00 |
| ⅞ | 0.80 | 2⅞ | 2.63 | 4⅞ | 4.46 | 6⅞ | 6.29 | 8⅞ | 8.12 |
| 1 | 0.91 | 3 | 2.74 | 5 | 4.57 | 7 | 6.40 | 9 | 8.23 |
| 1⅛ | 1.03 | 3⅛ | 2.86 | 5⅛ | 4.69 | 7⅛ | 6.52 | 9⅛ | 8.34 |
| 1¼ | 1.14 | 3¼ | 2.97 | 5¼ | 4.80 | 7¼ | 6.63 | 9¼ | 8.46 |
| 1⅜ | 1.26 | 3⅜ | 3.09 | 5⅜ | 4.91 | 7⅜ | 6.74 | 9⅜ | 8.57 |
| 1½ | 1.37 | 3½ | 3.20 | 5½ | 5.03 | 7½ | 6.86 | 9½ | 8.69 |
| 1⅝ | 1.49 | 3⅝ | 3.31 | 5⅝ | 5.14 | 7⅝ | 6.97 | 9⅝ | 8.80 |
| 1¾ | 1.60 | 3¾ | 3.43 | 5¾ | 5.26 | 7¾ | 7.09 | 9¾ | 8.92 |
| 1⅞ | 1.71 | 3⅞ | 3.54 | 5⅞ | 5.37 | 7⅞ | 7.20 | 9⅞ | 9.03 |
| 2 | 1.83 | 4 | 3.66 | 6 | 5.49 | 8 | 7.32 | 10 | 9.14 |

## Dry and Liquid Measurements

3 tsp. = 1 Tbl.  
4 Tbl. = ¼ cup  

1 ounce = 28.35 grams  
1 pound = 453.59 grams  

1 Tbl. = ½ fluid ounce  
1 cup = 8 fluid ounces  

1 Tbl. = 14.79 milliliters  
1 cup = 236.6 milliliters  
1 quart = 946.4 milliliters

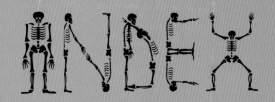

# INDEX